HAIR-RAISING HALLOWEEN

CREEPY COSTUMES

DIY ZOMBIES, GHOULS, AND MORE

by Mary Meinking

CAPSTONE PRESS
a capstone imprint

Blazers Books are published by Capstone Press,
1710 Roe Crest Drive, North Mankato, Minnesota 56003
www.mycapstone.com

Library of Congress Cataloging-in-Publication data
Names: Meinking, Mary, author.
Title: Creepy costumes: DIY zombies, ghouls, and more / by Mary
Meinking.
Description: North Mankato, Minnesota: Capstone Press, [2019] |
Series: Blazers. Hair-raising Halloween | Includes bibliographical
references and index. | Audience: Age 8. | Audience: Grades K to 3.
Identifiers: LCCN 2018005775 (print) | LCCN 2018021563 (ebook) |
ISBN 9781543530889 (eBook PDF) | ISBN 9781543530308
(library binding: alk. paper) | ISBN 9781543530346 (pbk.: alk. paper)
Subjects: LCSH: Halloween costumes—Juvenile literature.
Classification: LCC TT633 (ebook) | LCC TT633 .M45 2019 (print) |
DDC 646.4/78—dc23 LC record available at
https://lccn.loc.gov/2018005775

Editorial Credits
Mandy Robbins, editor; Juliette Peters, designer;
Morgan Walters, media researcher; Laura Manthe, production specialist;
Marcy Morin, scheduler; Sarah Schuette, photo stylist

Photo Credits
All images Capstone Studio: Karon Dubke

Design Elements
Shutterstock: Sasa Prudkov, Wandeaw

Printed and bound in the United States of America.
PA017

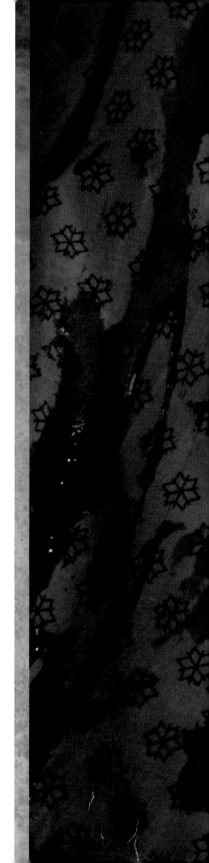

Table of Contents

SPOOK-TACULAR COSTUMES

Do you want your Halloween costume to freak out your friends this year? Create a look that will send everyone running.

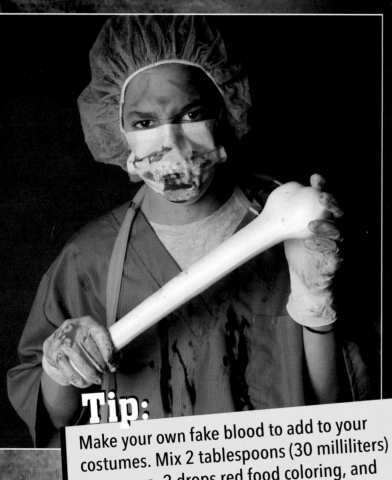

Tip:

Make your own fake blood to add to your costumes. Mix 2 tablespoons (30 milliliters) corn syrup, 2 drops red food coloring, and ¼ cup (60 mL) hot cocoa mix.

COSTUME BASICS

Push your costume's fright
factor with these tips.

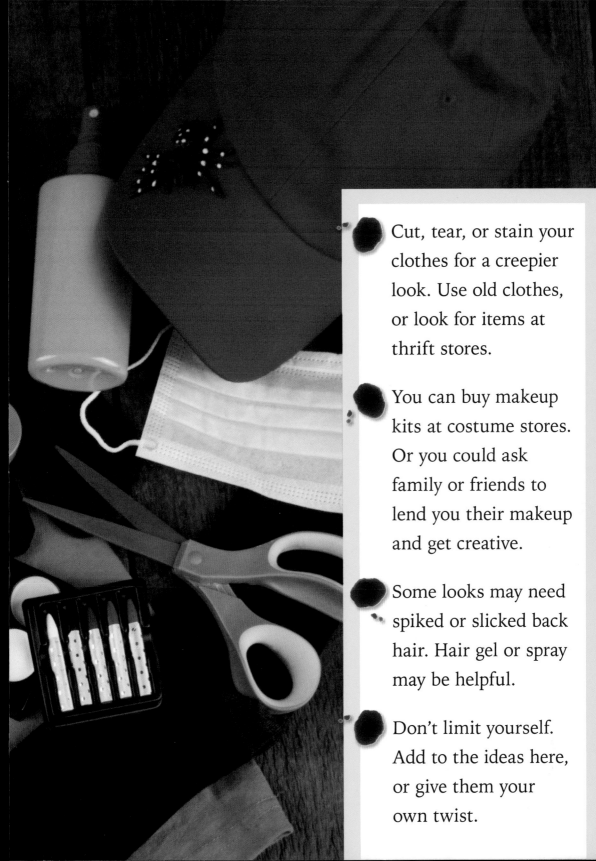

Cut, tear, or stain your clothes for a creepier look. Use old clothes, or look for items at thrift stores.

You can buy makeup kits at costume stores. Or you could ask family or friends to lend you their makeup and get creative.

Some looks may need spiked or slicked back hair. Hair gel or spray may be helpful.

Don't limit yourself. Add to the ideas here, or give them your own twist.

7

HEADLESS WONDER

Want to make your friends scream? Try carrying your head on a platter!

WHAT YOU NEED:

- ❏ a scissors
- ❏ an extra heavy disposable paper platter
- ❏ silver paint
- ❏ a paintbrush
- ❏ a backpack
- ❏ an adult's long raincoat
- ❏ gloves
- ❏ polyester stuffing
- ❏ safety pins
- ❏ industrial-strength glue
- ❏ lettuce and tomato

1. Cut a C-shape out of the side of the platter. It should fit around your neck.

2. Paint the platter. Let it dry.

3. Fill the backpack, gloves, and coat sleeves with stuffing.

4. Pin the gloves on the end of each sleeve.

5. Glue the gloves like they're holding the platter.

6. Slip on the backpack. Put the coat on with your head at chest level. Rest your chin on the platter.

7. Ask someone to button the coat around your head and add stuffing to fill the coat above you.

8. Glue lettuce and tomato to your platter for a funny twist.

MAN-EATING SHARK

Sharks have big appetites. Become a shark's latest meal for a scare-worthy costume!

WHAT YOU NEED:

- ❑ a large, gray hooded sweatshirt and sweatpants
- ❑ red, white, gray, and black felt
- ❑ a scissors
- ❑ fabric glue
- ❑ polyester stuffing
- ❑ fake blood

1. Turn the sweatshirt inside out. Cut out two pieces of red felt to match the flattened hood.

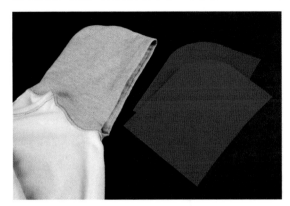

2. Cut out two rows of teeth from the white felt.

3. Cut a large white felt oval.

4. Cut out two 1-inch (2.5-centimeter) black felt circles for eyes.

5. Cut two 6- by 8-inch (15- by 20-cm) gray felt triangles for a fin.

11

6. Glue the teeth inside the hood.

7. Add stuffing inside the hood to fill the point.

8. Glue red felt inside the hood.

Tip:

Let the glue dry between each step. This will add more time but make a stronger costume.

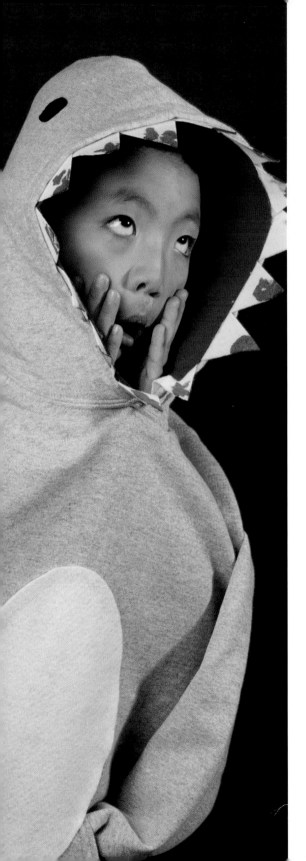

9. Cut a slit in the back of the sweatshirt. Glue two sides of the triangles together. Fill it with stuffing. Push the fin through the hole in the sweatshirt. Glue it securely.

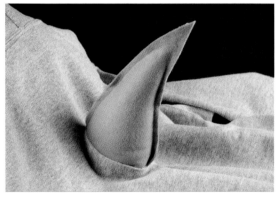

10. Glue black eyes outside on the hood. Glue the white oval to the stomach.

11. Wear the sweatpants and sweatshirt. Add fake blood to your neck and shark's teeth.

OOZING HEAD WOUND PATIENT

Be yourself—with a terrifying twist. Your brain is spilling out!

WHAT YOU NEED:

- ❏ **seam ripper**
- ❏ a red baseball cap (fit to your head, not adjustable)
- ❏ a bowl the size of cap
- ❏ plastic wrap
- ❏ a utility knife
- ❏ a tube of acrylic **caulk**
- ❏ caulk gun
- ❏ dark red acrylic paint
- ❏ paint brush
- ❏ a hospital gown
- ❏ rolls of cloth gauze
- ❏ fake blood

1. Use the seam ripper to remove the cap's brim.

2. Cover the bowl with wrap. Then place the cap on it.

3. Have an adult cut the tip off the caulk tube. Load the tube into the gun. Make squiggles over half the cap. Repeat on the other side. Let it dry overnight.

4. Paint the caulk "brain" with watered-down paint. Let dry.

5. Dress in the hospital gown and brain cap. Wrap gauze around the edge of the brain.

6. Wrap gauze around an arm and a leg. Drizzle fake blood all over the costume.

seam ripper—a sewing tool that cuts seams or threads

caulk—a waterproof paste that is applied to edges that need to be watertight

15

BLOOD-THIRSTY SURGEON

Be a surgeon with a secret—you're actually a vampire! Do you want to heal people, or are you looking for your next meal?

WHAT YOU NEED:

- ❏ hospital scrubs
- ❏ a plastic **stethoscope**
- ❏ plastic fangs
- ❏ a scissors
- ❏ a disposable surgical mask
- ❏ fake blood
- ❏ hair cap and rubber gloves (optional)

1. Put on the scrubs. Hang the stethoscope around your neck. Add the hair cap and rubber gloves if you have them.

2. Put in the plastic fangs. Cut slits in the surgical mask for the fangs to poke through. Put on the mask.

3. Drizzle blood from the fangs and on the mask. Add more blood on the scrubs and gloves.

Freaky Fact:

The largest group of people dressed like vampires numbered 1,039. They met on September 30, 2011, at Kings Dominion Theme Park in Doswell, Virginia.

stethoscope—a medical instrument used by doctors and nurses to listen to the sounds from a patient's heart and lungs

SKELETON PIRATE

Give your pirate costume this eerie twist. You'll look like you're back from the bottom of the sea.

WHAT YOU NEED:

- ❑ a paint brush
- ❑ white fabric paint
- ❑ a black sweatshirt and sweatpants
- ❑ black gloves
- ❑ scissors
- ❑ a red T-shirt
- ❑ tall black socks
- ❑ red and black striped fabric, 10 by 48 inches (24.4 by 122 cm) long
- ❑ white and black face paint

1. Paint rib and armbones on the sweatshirt and leg bones on the pants. Paint hand bones on the gloves. Let everything dry.

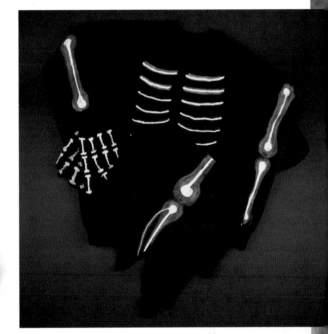

2. Cut the arms off the T-shirt. Cut down the middle of the front to make it a vest.

3. Cut the pants off at the knee in a zigzag pattern.

4. Put on the sweatshirt, pants, and socks. Put on the vest over top of them.

5. Cut the striped fabric into two strips. One should be 4 inches (10 cm) wide and the other 6 inches (15 cm) wide. Tie the thinner fabric strip around your waist. Tie the wider fabric strip around your head.

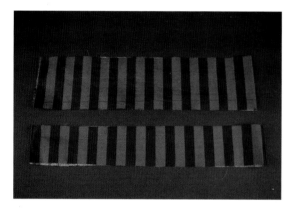

6. Paint your face and neck white. Paint the skull features with black. Put on the gloves.

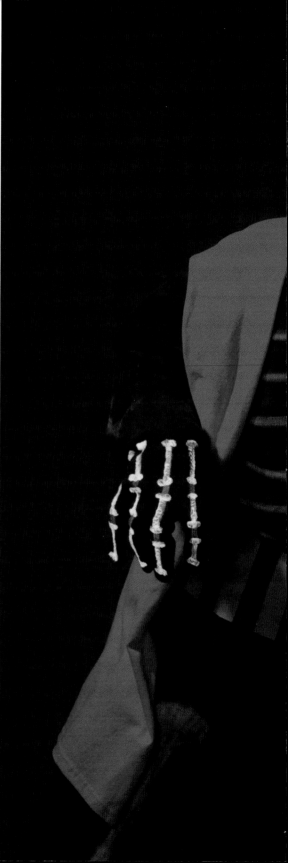

WEREWOLF QUARTERBACK

Howl with school spirit as you throw a winning touchdown. Or use your super speed to run into the end zone!

WHAT YOU NEED:

- ❏ a turtleneck
- ❏ a football jersey
- ❏ a brown wig (optional)
- ❏ brown and black face paint
- ❏ fake fangs
- ❏ brown fake fur
- ❏ safety pins
- ❏ a football

1. Put on the turtleneck first and then the jersey.

2. If your hair is long enough, spike it so it sticks up. Otherwise you can wear a wig.

3. Draw a **widow's peak** on your forehead with the brown paint. Fill it in with short lines.

4. Color in bushy eyebrows and a beard.

5. Paint the tip of your nose black. Put in the fangs.

6. Cut two rectangles of fur twice the size of the back of your hand. Pin them to the inside of your turtleneck sleeve.

7. Pin another strip of fur around your neck. Then grab your football and hit the field!

widow's peak—a V-shaped hairline in the middle of the forehead

ZOMBIE BASEBALL PLAYER

Did you catch a baseball to your head? Become a zombie baseball player who really uses his head.

WHAT YOU NEED:

- ❏ a scissors
- ❏ an old baseball uniform
- ❏ a baseball hat and glove
- ❏ dirt
- ❏ fake blood
- ❏ a serrated knife (a knife that has teeth like a saw)
- ❏ a rubber baseball
- ❏ industrial-strength glue
- ❏ white, gray, and black, face paint
- ❏ liquid latex

1. Cut slits in the uniform. Rub the uniform and hat with dirt. Splatter them with blood.

2. Ask an adult to cut the baseball in half. Stick it to the side of the hat with glue, and let it dry.

3. Paint your face and neck white. Blend in black and gray around your eyes and under your cheekbones.

4. Place blobs of latex on your face, arms, and legs. Pull and pick at the latex until it looks like scabs. Dab fake blood onto the scabs.

5. Put on the uniform and hat. Add fake blood wherever you think looks best.

MONSTER ATTACK

Let a monster carry you around the neighborhood this Halloween. Your neighbors will lock their doors in fear!

1. Wear black pants and shoes.

2. Cut a slit in the back of the pajamas large enough for your head to fit through. Fill the body and legs with stuffing.

3. Fill the backpack with polyester stuffing.

4. Put the mask on the foam head. Put the foam head on the PVC pipe. Stick it into the backpack so that it will be above your own head when you put the backpack on.

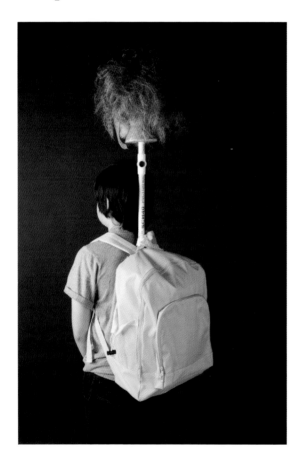

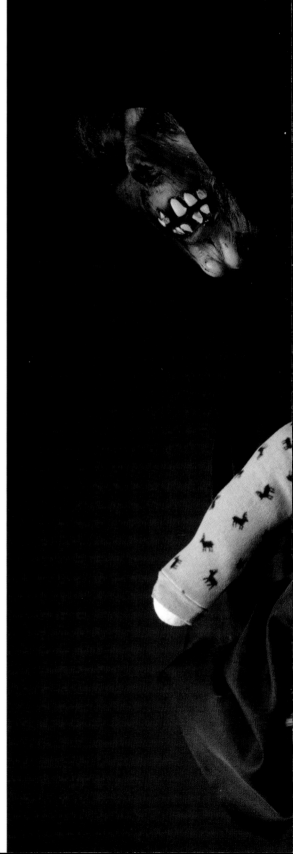

5. With the backpack on, put on the black coat with your arms through the armholes.

6. Put the hood over the monster head. Stick your head out between a couple open button holes.

7. Slip the pajamas over your head. Add any stuffing if needed.

8. Put on the monster gloves, and hold the baby.

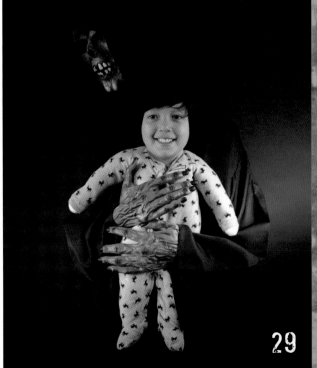

GLOSSARY

caulk (KAWK)—a waterproof paste that is applied to edges that need to be watertight

forehead (FOR-hed)—the top part of your face between your hair and your eyes

seam ripper (SEEM RIP-uhr)—a sewing tool that cuts seams or threads

serrated (SER-ay-tid)—describes a sharp object that has teeth like a saw

stethoscope (STETH-uh-skope)—a medical instrument used by doctors and nurses to listen to the sounds from a patient's heart, lungs, and other areas

surgeon (SUR-juhn)—a doctor who performs operations

widow's peak (WI-dohs PEEK)—a V-shaped hairline in the middle of the forehead

READ MORE

Besel, Jennifer M. *A Halloween Drawing Spooktacular!*
First Facts. North Mankato, Minn.: Capstone Press, 2014.

Loh-Hagan, Virginia. *Haunted House. D.I.Y.* Make it
Happen. Ann Arbor, Mich.: Cherry Lake Publishing, 2016.

Owen, Ruth. *The Halloween Gross-Out Guide.* DIY for Boys.
New York: PowerKids Press, 2014.

INTERNET SITES

Use FactHound to find Internet sites related to
this book.

Visit *www.facthound.com*

Just type in 9781543530308 and go!

INDEX